SHOULDER
TO SHOULDER

THE HORTON COLLECTION

SHOULDER TO SHOULDER

Bicycle Racing in the Age of Anquetil

Boulder, Colorado

▼velopress®

3002 Sterling Circle, Suite 100 • Boulder, Colorado 80301-2338 USA
(303) 440-0601 • Fax (303) 444-6788 • E-mail velopress@competitorgroup.com

Distributed in the United States and Canada by Ingram Publisher Services

A Cataloging-in-Publication record for this book is available from the Library of Congress.
ISBN 978-1-937715-36-6

For information on purchasing VeloPress books, please call (800) 811-4210, ext. 2138, or visit www.velopress.com.

This paper meets the requirements of ANSI/NISO Z39.48-1992 (Permanence of Paper).

Photo retouching by Elizabeth Riley
Design by Vicki Hopewell

15   16   17 / 10   9   8   7   6   5   4   3   2   1

■ ■ ■

On the cover:
Jacques Anquetil and Rick van Looy, 1963 Tour of Sardinia
Anquetil and Van Looy share a light moment during stage 3

FIRST EDITION
This first edition includes a limited run of 200 hardbound copies in custom slipcases, numbered and signed by the authors, and 26 hardbound copies in custom slipcases, lettered A to Z, signed by the authors, each containing an original pre–World War II racing photograph.

For Trevor

INTRODUCTION

It is in some ways ironic that throughout most of the hip, happening, swinging '60s, cycling's most public and accomplished face was that of Jacques Anquetil, a cerebral, calculating, and distant Frenchman. Born in Normandy, France's northern bulwark against the English, Anquetil developed a shrewd eye for profit as he worked on his family's strawberry farm, and although he was frequently painted as a bon vivant later in his career—a man who would call for roast pheasant and another glass of champagne the night before a critical stage in the Tour de France—he never strayed far from his farming roots in the way he would coolly survey the landscape before a race and create his tactical plan on how—or even whether—to win it. He was hardly the portrait of a carefree, pop-a-pill-and-let-the-good-times-roll '60s archetype.

But in the same way that the Beatles could never have defined the music and mores of the '50s (the Rolling Stones are another matter), Anquetil was the essential figure to bring cycling out of the Fausto Coppi era. Without Anquetil's style and success, his candor in interviews, and his exotic looks in every photo, cycling would have spent another decade on the grimy black-and-white back pages of local newspapers rather than erupting onto the four-color covers of national magazines. Indeed, we all would have had to await the arrival of Eddy Merckx, and 10 years would have been lost.

This is not to say that there were no other stars, no other cycling personalities to capture our attention and affections as the new decade dawned. This book is full of them. There was Tom Simpson, the transplanted Englishman with an earnest yet slightly befuddled mien who crossed the Channel and became a sort of honorary Frenchman in his veneration for the Tour and its traditions (mastering the language did not hurt his cause).

There was Federico Bahamontes, a lanky Spaniard who could climb into the clouds on a trail of vapor and could barely descend a mountain without a crash. His erratic behavior and puzzling inconsistency were adorable, and he had plenty of fans.

There was, of course, Rik van Looy—Rik II, following the reign of Rik van Steenbergen—the Emperor who steamrolled his way to a crushing total of 492 career victories. If you wanted to hang a picture of cycling success on your wall back then, Van Looy was your boy, front and center.

Competent, great champions, one and all. Some of them, like Van Looy, a little thuggish, but that only added to their attractive danger.

But none had the panache of Anquetil. None carried themselves in a way that made them untouchable. None were ever going to be pursued relentlessly by the paparazzi to capture their dashing elegance for the style pages of the monthly glossies.

The fact is, all of them were cyclists. Great cyclists, to be sure, but cyclists first, athletes second, and public figures barely.

Anquetil was essential for cycling because of all his cycling contemporaries, only he had the imperial bearing, the jaw-dropping presence, the disregard for convention that our modern heroes need to stand apart. He was the perfect man for his time because he strolled onto the athletic stage at exactly the moment when the athlete's presence in society was being redefined.

That redefinition of the athlete's image was, of course, entirely due to the explosion of new media in the '60s and its voracious appetite for fresh stars. The rapidly improving technology—color TV, four-color weekly newsmagazines, faster film emulsions, lighter and more portable cameras— doted on the photogenic and witty and shunned the unattractive dullards, no matter how accomplished.

It was an era for the dashing and cosmopolitan, a time for the wry insider. The athletes who captured hearts were not the journeymen, the bricklayers who could persevere through the muck to stand on a rain-soaked podium; they were quite the opposite, almost indifferent to the commotion they left in their wake—still determined to win, but to win with style. They all had a touch of James Bond.

They were athletes like Jean-Claude Killy, a giant slalom skier of unimaginable speed, hurtling down snow-covered rock faces with reckless abandon, nearly out of control, poles akimbo, skimming across the finish line on one ski, the other pinwheeling away in a cloud of snow. He married an actress. He was sponsored by Moët & Chandon. He melted American hearts with his rugged looks and charmingly accented English.

They were athletes like Jackie Stewart, the wee Scotsman, successor to compatriot Jim Clark in Formula 1, but a better man for the media than Clark because not only did he have the accent, not only did he have the style—long hair, big sunglasses, a corduroy Breton hat—but he also had the vocabulary for the press to perfectly describe the fragmenting terrors of his profession and then the aplomb to slip into the narrow aluminum shell of his car and race off to victory.

They were athletes like Giacomo Agostini, a suave northern Italian with movie-star looks, a Grand Prix motorcycle racer of irresistible charm who would defy death in every turn as he pushed his snarling bike deeper into the corners, then sweep into the winner's circle and pull off his helmet to reveal a stunning mass of perfectly coiffed

3

black hair and a wry, gleaming grin before greeting the press in three languages.

And there was Anquetil, who gnawed over every detail but never let the public see him do it.

In these pages we have a revealing presentation of our two Anquetils: Anquetil the champion bicycle racer and Anquetil the modern athlete. His credentials in both worlds are impeccable. As a cycling champion, he was, as we all know, the first to win the Tour de France five times. He set the hour record in 1956 and won the Grand Prix des Nations nine times and brought that exacting time trial skill to bear in every road race, pressuring his adversaries with relentless speed. He skipped the Tour de France in 1960 in favor of the Giro d'Italia and went on to win it, the first Frenchman to do so. He won it again in 1964, the same year he won his fifth Tour title and one of his first classics, Ghent–Wevelgem. He was not a rider who sought to win everything, but he invariably won the races that mattered to him, whether the motivation was prestige or money, and he always won with style.

To attest to Anquetil's credentials as a modern athlete, we have additional images to admire: Anquetil the press favorite (page 71), the elegant homebody (pages 74–75), the tousled hero (page 76).

Of these, it may be the latter portrait that is most arresting. It embodies all that we admire in our athletes and what we imagine for them. The sculpted cheeks, the casual mop of hair, a look in the eyes of interest and anticipation but also utter confidence. He stands reviewing the finishing times in the individual time trial for stage 20 of the 1962 Tour. Until this day, he has not led the Tour. Instead, he has waited for this day of the time trial to make his move. He has finished his race, and now he stands to the side, carefully calculating the other riders' intervals. His claim on the yellow jersey, and the Tour title, depends on no one bettering his time, and so there is some anxiety. And yet he knows, with an athletic certainty that few others may ever have, that no one can match him.

Jacques Anquetil

1959 Paris–Roubaix

Monsieur Chrono brings his celebrated time trial form to the spring classic

Fausto Coppi, Biagio Cavanna, and Jacques Anquetil

· · ·

1953 Trofeo Baracchi

Young espoir Anquetil meets the Campionissimo and his blind soigneur at Coppi's estate

Jacques Anquetil

* * *

Mont-Saint-Aignan
Anquetil at his parents' farmhouse with his mother, Marie

Jacques Anquetil

⁂

National Service, 1954

On September 22, Anquetil begins two years of compulsory service

Raymond Poulidor, Mino Baracchi, and Jacques Anquetil

· · ·

1963 Trofeo Baracchi

The favored French stars debate the reasons for their defeat as Baracchi worriedly mediates

Rik van Looy and Rik van Steenbergen
◦ ◦ ◦

1963 Berlin Six-Day
Belgium's two Riks compete for the first time as a team

Pino Cerami

• • •

1960 Paris–Roubaix

The race winner on his way from the podium

Midstage Refreshment

※ ※ ※

1961 Giro d'Italia

Riders make an opportunistic grab for drinks along the route

Stage Transfer

1961 Giro d'Italia

Team cars, complete with bicycles, being loaded for transfer to Sardinia

Gerard Thelin and Raymond Poulidor

1963 Tour de France
Poulidor finishes stage 12 in Toulouse with a broken handlebar

Tom Simpson

∎ ∎ ∎

Tour de France

Simpson hams it up at a stage start; the fingers of the actual accordionist are visible below his

Rik van Looy

1962 Tour of Flanders

The always confident 1961 world champion heads to the Flanders podium

Kas and Ferry Teams

• • •

1964 Tour de France

Spanish riders sing a few tunes before the stage start

Jean Stablinski

· · ·

Date Unknown
A dramatic photo of a nonplussed Stablinski, post-crash at the hospital

Jean Graczyk

• • •

1960 Tour of Flanders

Graczyk, a sprinter, grapples with Le Ronde's cobbled climbs

Rudi Altig

* * *

Unknown Race, 1960
An accomplished track rider, Altig was just beginning his pro road career in 1960

Arthur de Cabooter

- - -

1960 Tour of Flanders

De Cabooter celebrates his surprising win over big names Jean Graczyk and Rik van Looy

Jan Janssen

⋯

1964 World Championships

Janssen dons the rainbow jersey following victory over Vittorio Adorni and Raymond Poulidor

Jean-Pierre van Haverbeke

• • •

1963 Grand Prix d'Orchies
Already hurt at the start of the season, Van Haverbeke crashes heavily at this 178-km criterium

24

Willy Butzen

. . .

1960 Tour of Flanders
Butzen crashes out of the race

Second Crash

1962 Paris–Roubaix
A small group recovers following the second crash of the day

Diego Ronchini

1963 Giro d'Italia

Ronchini fights to hold his overall lead on the unmade road to La Spezia

Rik van Looy and Albertus Geldermans

• • •

1961 Paris–Roubaix

Van Looy, the victor, in full flight chasing Geldermans on the cobbles; Geldermans finished fifth

28

Charly Gaul

* * *

1961 Giro d'Italia
The Angel of the Mountains takes on the Passo dello Stelvio solo

Raymond Poulidor

• • •

1971 Paris–Roubaix

Poulidor, never a winner of Paris–Roubaix, heads to an 11th place finish

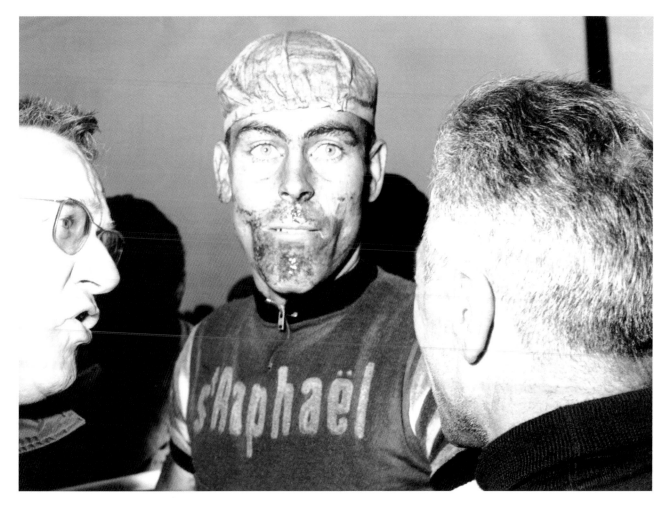

Jo de Roo

1963 Paris–Tours
Following his victory in the Giro di Lombardia, De Roo takes the autumn double in Tours

Italo Zilioli

* * *

1963 Giro d'Italia

Zilioli finished second on the 128-km climb to Belluno Nevegal

Guido Reybrouck

* * *

1964 Giro d'Italia

Following this crash, neopro Reybrouck remounted, eventually completing the Giro 88th of 97 finishers

Walter Serena

• • •

1956 Giro d'Italia

On a day described as "brutally hot," Serena stuffs his pockets in anticipation of a long day

Unknown Rider

* * *

1962 Giro d'Italia
One way to open a bottle midrace

Vito Taccone

* * *

1963 Giro d'Italia

In an unusual photo from above, Taccone refreshes at a fountain without dismounting

Peloton

∗ ∗ ∗

1962 Circuit des Boucles de la Seine

Riders fill bottles at a fountain before rejoining the race

Raymond Poulidor

■ ■ ■

1969 Tour de France

Poulidor's mechanic hangs out of the team car's cut-down door to make a derailleur adjustment

Jacques Anquetil

1962 Paris–Roubaix

Anquetil leads his teammates on reconnaissance before the race

Raymond Poulidor

■ ■ ■

1961 Paris–Roubaix

Poulidor and his motorpacer pre-ride the course in training

Miguel Poblet

* * *

1961 Giro d'Italia
Poblet takes the 115-km stage 1 in driving rain

Salvador Rosa

■ ■ ■

1961 Giro d'Italia
Rosa finished 63rd overall, 2:11:47 behind, his most notable professional result

Peloton

1962 Giro d'Italia
A bar under assault by the gregari

43

Tom Simpson
■ ■ ■

1964 Tour de France
Pre-Tour in Rennes, Simpson borrows a bagpipe for a blow

Jean Stablinski and Jacques Anquetil

■ ■ ■

1962

Stablinski and Anquetil prepare for a cold training ride, using newspapers as insulation

Joseph Groussard

• • •

1962 National de la Route

Winner Joseph with his brother Georges (right), signing post-race autographs

Fernand Delort

• • •

1962 Bordeaux–Paris

Delort stands for a midrace rubdown; he abandoned the race shortly thereafter

Cool Refreshment

• • •

1963 Giro d'Italia
The tailgunner grabs a handful of snow on the climb to Lavarone

Jean Stablinski

1963 Critérium du Dauphiné Libéré
Stage 4 winner Stablinski with a bottle of Perrier in a race ultimately won by Jacques Anquetil

Rudi Altig

* * *

1964 Tour de France

Altig enjoys a bite during a quiet moment on stage 20

Peloton

• • •

1961 Giro d'Italia

The race makes its way through the Dolomites

Rik van Looy

* * *

1962 Giro d'Italia

Caught in a snowstorm 39 km before the stage 14 finish, Van Looy and 56 other riders abandoned

52

Henri Anglade

• • •

1962 Giro d'Italia

Anglade is steadied by Jean Bobet at the stage 14 finish in Passo Rolle

Unknown Rider

• • •

1962 Critérium des As
A bad ending in the "Race of Aces"

54

Peugeot BP Team

* * *

1962 Circuit des Boucles de la Seine
A mechanical and an injury

Armand Desmet

* * *

1962 Giro d'Italia
Desmet doggedly rides to the snow-struck finish of stage 14; he would complete the Giro 10th overall

56

Federico Bahamontes

1962 Critérium du Dauphiné Libéré
Bahamontes displays his climbing form on stage 5 to Gap; he finished fourth overall

Unknown Terrot Rider

∗ ∗ ∗

1963 Paris–Nice

Dazed but intact, the Terrot rider watches Seamus Elliott ride off in the distance

Federico Bahamontes

1961 Giro d'Italia

Bahamontes crashes on stage 14, ceding the mountains jersey to Vito Taccone and abandoning the race

Tom Simpson and Gastone Nencini

. . .

1962 Four Days of Dunkirk
Pre-race portrait

Roger Rivière and Raymond Poulidor

1962 Mercier-Hutchinson Team
Rivière (left) and Poulidor (second from left) ponder their chances in a card game with teammates

Albertus Geldermans

1962 Paris–Nice
Geldermans chugs up the snowy road above Saint-Étienne on stage 5a; he eventually abandoned

Rudi Altig

1964 Tour de France

Altig and Jo de Roo grab treats; in theory, shopkeepers were reimbursed by the race organizer after these raids

Alberto Assirelli

• • •

1962 Giro d'Italia

Assirelli loosens a toe strap following his stage 20 victory in Saint-Vincent

Jacques Anquetil

1963 Critérium du Dauphiné Libéré
Anquetil hoists his bike over the gate at a rail crossing

Jean Stablinski

• • •

1963 French National Championships
On his way to a repeat victory, Stablinski channels the power of a massive crowd

Jacques Anquetil

* * *

1963 Critérium du Dauphiné Libéré
Anquetil, always intensely conscious of his appearance, smooths his hair before ascending the podium

Tom Simpson

1963 Tour du Var

Simpson celebrates his stage 1 victory at Frejus; he finished the race second overall

Rudi Altig

1963 Paris–Nice

Altig in the leader's jersey, center; Jacques Anquetil is on the far right

Jean Stablinski

• • •

1963 Paris–Nice

Stablinski, the 1962 world champion, gets assistance from Jacques Anquetil and a local to pin on his race numbers

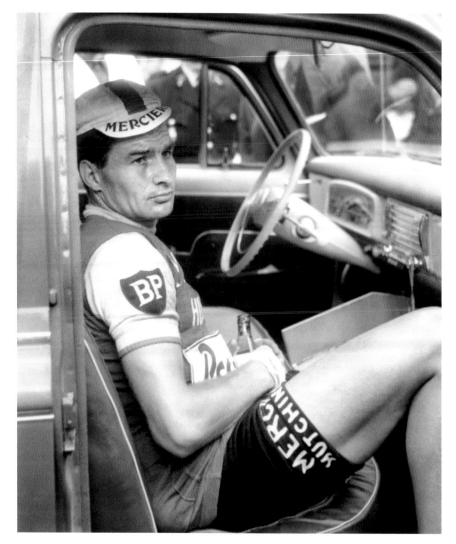

Raymond Poulidor

. . .

1963 Critérium du Dauphiné Libéré

Poulidor post-stage in his team car; the seven-stage race was ultimately won by Jacques Anquetil

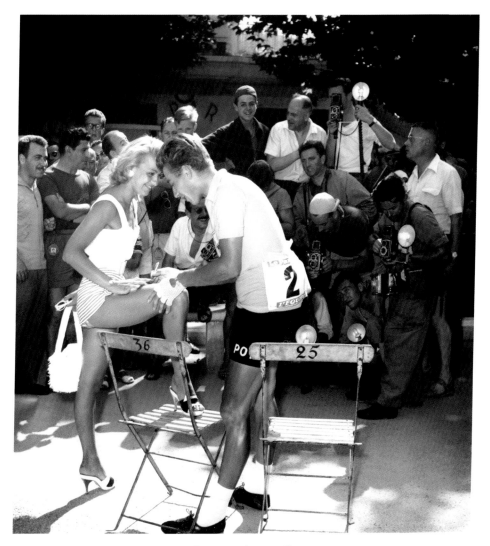

Jacques Anquetil

• • •

1957 Tour de France

Anquetil obliges with an unorthodox autograph

Jacques Anquetil

* * *

1963 Critérium des As

Anquetil, four-time winner of the Race of Aces, on his way to victory in 1963

Peloton

• • •

1963 Giro d'Italia

Stage 10, La Spezia to Asti; Vito Taccone won the stage and Diego Ronchini kept the maglia rosa

Janine and Jacques Anquetil

Saint-Adrien, 1966
Anquetil and his wife display their speedboat style

Jacques and Janine Anquetil

· · ·

At Home, 1966
The Anquetils pull out a few of Jacques's jerseys for the press

Jacques Anquetil

. . .

1962 Tour de France
A portrait of the champion

Jacques Anquetil

• • •

Circa 1957

Though Anquetil's all-out efforts were sometimes theatrical, they were very real—and legendary

Jo de Roo

* * *

1963 Giro di Lombardia

Race winner De Roo climbs an unpaved sector

Gastone Nencini and Hans Schleuniger

· · ·

1960 Tour de France

Maillot jaune Nencini with the then–lanterne rouge; Schleuniger ultimately finished 80th of 81

80

Jean Graczyk

* * *

1962 Paris–Roubaix

Graczyk, an expert at solo attacks, goes on the offensive

Henri Anglade

- - -

1960 Tour de France

Anglade crashed at Mas d'Azil, stage 12, but ultimately captured eighth overall

82

Jacques Anquetil

1963 Critérium National de la Route

Winner Anquetil in the race known today as the Critérium International; Poulidor, naturally, finished second

Louison Bobet

* * *

1961 Dreux Cyclocross

In the twilight of his cycling career, Bobet ascends a steep hillside

Peloton

◦ ◦ ◦

1964 Tour de France
Food grab, stage 11

Federico Bahamontes

■ ■ ■

1963 Tour de France
The Eagle of Toledo briefly held the overall lead but had to settle for second and the mountains jersey

Ivan Levacic

■ ■ ■

1961 Tour de l'Avenir
In the Avenir's first running, Levacic cools off during a hot stage at Saint-Étienne.

Miguel Poblet and Rik van Looy

1961 Giro d'Italia
Van Looy puffs a cigarette given to him by Gino Bartali

Les Chasseurs

• • •

1963 Paris–Tours

Two hunters pause to watch the October classic stream by

Peloton

• • •

1964 Tour de France
Fans "share" food during stage 11

Benoni Beheyt

• • •

1963 World Championships
Beheyt barely edged out his fellow Belgian Rik van Looy for the win in Ronse, Belgium

Raymond Poulidor

1964 Giro di Lombardia

Poulidor gets a quick bike change in the Race of the Falling Leaves

Jacques Goddet

• • •

1964 Tour de France

The Tour director keeps watch in his customary pith helmet and safari garb

Unknown Mercier Rider

■ ■ ■

1964 Tour de France

Somewhere between stages 10a and 10b, the only thing this rider kept was his shorts

Gastone Nencini

* * *

1959 Paris–Tours

Nencini gets a wheel change from what must be the most cheerful race support car ever made

Liberia-Grammont Team

. . .

1962 Circuit des Boucles de la Seine
A variation on today's "sticky bottle" method of pushing a rider back to the front

Jacques Anquetil

■ ■ ■

1963 Tour de France

Under the intense scrutiny of the press photographers, Anquetil attacks the stage 19 time trial

Antonio Uliana

∎ ∎ ∎

1959 Tour de Suisse

Uliana, a lifetime domestique, rides to victory on stage 4

Vittorio Adorni
* * *

1968 World Championships
Adorni celebrates his runaway win over Herman van Springel (9:50 in arrears) and Michele Dancelli (10:18 back)

Unknown Rider

* * *

1962 Vuelta a España

A Faema rider in trouble; of 90 starters, only 48 finished the 1962 Vuelta's 17 stages

Benoni Beheyt

■ ■ ■

1964 Paris–Roubaix

1963 world champion Beheyt skirts the cobbles on his way to a second-place finish

Arnaldo Pambianco

■ ■ ■

1960 Giro d'Italia

Atop the Gavia Pass, Pambianco prepares insulation for the drop into Bormio

Rudi Altig and Pierre Everaert

1960 Tour of Germany

Runner-up Altig (left) and stage winner Everaert pose post-race following a 303-km stage from Brackwede to Giessen

Jean-Marie Cieleska

■ ■ ■

1959 Bordeaux–Paris

Cieleska gets an assist from his cigarette-smoking, Chucks-wearing mechanic; Cieleska finished eighth

André Darrigade

. . .

1959 Circuit Daumesnil

Darrigade chases his derny to a third-place finish

Eddy Merckx and Jacques Anquetil

■ ■ ■

1969 Critérium de Caen

A passing of the torch

Laundry Day

• • •

Giro d'Italia

Wool jerseys, wool shorts, stiff chamois—cycling was a rough, itchy business

NOTES

Page 5 Anquetil in full flight, displaying inimitable souplesse. On this day he would finish 24th, 3:19 behind race winner Noël Foré. Better results were to come.

Page 6 On November 3, 1953, the day before the Baracchi Trophy race, young hopeful Jacques Anquetil met with Fausto Coppi at Coppi's home in Novi Ligure. Coppi was still compiling major victories, and Anquetil's career had barely started. Still, this photo can be viewed as a meeting of cycling's past and future, with a new era about to begin.

Page 7 Anquetil shared his family's farmhouse with his parents, Ernest and Marie, and his brother, Philippe.

Page 8 Anquetil served as a gunner in the 406th artillery regiment, but the strangest story of his military service is that the army was responsible for pushing him into setting the hour record in 1956. He had already made two failed attempts to beat Fausto Coppi's mark, but following his second attempt he received a telegram from his commander urging him to try once more. On June 29, 1956, he set a new record of 46.159 km under the watchful eye of his captain.

Page 9 From 1944 to 1991, the Trofeo Baracchi was a fixture on the pro calendar. Set up as a time trial for two-man teams, this November invitational was generally viewed as the closing event of the season. In 1963, countrymen Poulidor and Anquetil joined forces and were the odds-on favorites to win. Although the finish was close, the French stars had to settle for second, losing to Joseph Velly and Joseph Novales by 9 seconds over a two-and-one-half-hour stretch.

Page 10 A historic moment, when two of Belgium's giants ride for the first time as a team. The venue was the Deutschlandhalle, Berlin.

Page 11 In the greatest victory of his 18-year professional career, Cerami won alone at the Roubaix velodrome, with a margin of 14 seconds over Tino Sabbadini of France.

Page 12 A fully loaded drink truck was an instant target for the peloton, especially one stocked with a favored midrace beverage. Forget energy drinks; Coca-Cola was the real deal, in part due to its caffeine boost. The glee is apparent in the eyes of the riders as they strip the truck of its inventory. The boy standing in the field with his father, however, is not so sure about the situation.

Page 13 Stage races can be logistical puzzles. While the publicity photos tend to show riders sitting comfortably in airplanes or trains, there are many parts to the moving circus. Here the team cars head across the Tyrrhenian Sea for stage 3.

Page 14 While this finish at the Toulouse velodrome looks carefree, it speaks to Poulidor's bike-handling skills; not everyone could deal with such a catastrophic failure so casually.

Page 15 Tom Simpson was always willing to oblige the Tour's press photographers. In this artfully composed shot, Simpson appears to be warbling his own creation, while most traces of the real musician to Simpson's left have vanished.

Page 16 About the only thing better for a Belgian than winning the Ronde van Vlaanderen is winning it while wearing the jersey of the world champion. Rik van Looy won in grand fashion with a solo victory, 9 seconds ahead of a thundering chase group.

Page 17 It's the morning of stage 2, when anything is possible. Why not start the day with a rousing round of songs?

Page 18 Stablinski, the son of Polish immigrants, turned professional at age 21 and rode for 10 years on Anquetil's teams. A rift between them, caused by a newspaper article written by Anquetil, saw him move to Raymond Poulidor's Mercier team, where he rode for one year before retiring at the end of 1968.

Page 19 Graczyk was a threat to win in every race, particularly if it was grindingly hard and ended in a sprint. At the 1960 Ronde van Vlaanderen, Graczyk almost grabbed victory. Unfortunately for him, second place was his spot for the day.

Page 20 Rudi Altig's muscular track roots dominate this shot from his first year as a road pro. He would go on to win the

Vuelta a España in 1962, the world championships in 1966, multiple grand tour stages and classics, and the German national championship.

Page 21 No one looks happier about the unexpected outcome than the victor himself.

Page 22 The 1964 world's, held in Sallanches, France, was a fierce battle that came down to three strong riders: Jan Janssen, Vittorio Adorni, and Raymond Poulidor. In this photo, the newly crowned champion is seen without his trademark rectangular tinted glasses, which he had to remove to pull on the rainbow jersey.

Page 23 While the circumstance is unfortunate, this picture captures many details, down to a cookie visible in Van Haverbeke's pocket. A domestique's life is rarely glamorous.

Page 24 Willy Butzen raced his six-season professional career as a domestique on teams sponsored by Dr. Mann, a producer of patent medicines. The Mann teams, often cosponsored by Grundig, were small-budget affairs, and the monetary rewards for soldiers like Butzen were exceedingly modest.

Page 25 The desire to be at the front of the field at Paris–Roubaix is intense, but one slight misstep can cause riders to fall. Fortunately, this crash did not result in any riders dropping from the race.

Page 26 Italy's Diego Ronchini, here resplendent in the maglia rosa, grinds up a climb in stage 9. Ronchini claimed, lost, and reclaimed the jersey through the first two weeks and valiantly held it for 10 days in total. His undoing came in the final two days in the mountains, where he lost the lead for good during stage 18. He paid dearly for his earlier efforts, conceding more than 10 minutes in the final four stages to eventual race winner Franco Balmamion.

Page 27 The race has started to sort out: Van Looy and Geldermans's attack has stretched out the field, and the snaking line behind them is composed mostly of press motos and team cars.

Page 28 The legendary climber from Luxembourg is off the front on the ascent of the Stelvio. He was the first over the climb and went on to win the stage.

Page 29 Poulidor leads a tight group of muddy riders as the field toils away.

Page 30 Get this man a towel! De Roo is pictured after winning a nine-man dash for the line at the rainy 1963 edition of Paris–Tours. Second-place Tom Simpson and third-place Raymond Poulidor rounded out the podium.

Page 31 As a professional rider, Zilioli won 58 races in his 15 seasons as a pro, including five stages at the Giro. Although he ascended the final podium of the Giro on four occasions, the top step ultimately eluded him. The field dress of the two Alpini behind Zilioli, members of Italy's elite mountain military, adds an exotic flavor to this image.

Page 32 Welcome to the pro ranks, Mr. Reybrouck! Here we find neopro Reybrouck isolated from the peloton after crashing at the 1964 Giro. He walks alone down the road, face bloodied, one hand hauling his bike, the other lifting his wheel in the air. Later that year he won Paris–Tours, a race he would claim three times in his career. An all-rounder, he won 13 grand tour stages among the Giro, Tour, and Vuelta. Other key wins included Züri–Metzgete (1964), the Belgium national road championship (1966), and the Amstel Gold race (1969).

Page 33 Contrary to what this photo implies, no stages of the 1956 Giro were run at night. Instead, the contrast between the rider and the background is due to the photographer's flash

overpowering the film emulsion and preventing any detail behind Serena from registering. The term for this phenomenon is "reciprocity failure," but let's just enjoy the results in this striking image.

Page 34 Sometimes a proper opener for your bottle is just not available in the middle of a race.

Page 35 Spin this fascinating photo 90 degrees clockwise and the content become apparent: a rider taking a break to run some cool water over his head. Interestingly, Taccone was often impugned for his poor bike-handling skills, though he seems to be doing fine here. He rode as a professional for 10 seasons, winning the 1961 Giro di Lombardia and seven stages at the Giro d'Italia.

Page 36 A candid shot of domestiques at work.

Page 37 With his right hand working the lever, Poulidor shows his mechanic the problem with his Simplex derailleur, a somewhat more fragile device than the stalwart Campagnolo gear changers of the time.

Page 38 Starting a tradition that continues today, teams in the '60s began reviewing the fabled course of Paris–Roubaix a few days before the race. This photograph captures a particularly muddy section. Look closely at the firepower in the photo: Anquetil, De Roo, Stablinski, and Graczyk, among others. What a team!

Page 39 Sporting fastidiously clean clothes and what look to be new shoes, Poulidor prepares for the slop of Paris–Roubaix on a reconnaissance ride.

Page 40 The intensity of the storm is easily visible in the size of the splashes of the raindrops on the road.

Page 41 Rosa rode six seasons as a pro, four of them with the fabled Faema team.

Page 42 With some degree of order, a group of domestiques has left their bicycles neatly on their sides as they stop briefly to grab refreshments.

Page 43 Simpson takes up a new instrument; the expressions of his fellow musicians indicate he has yet to master its nuances.

Page 44 Defiantly stylish in knickers and argyle socks, Stablinski and Anquetil demonstrate one way to keep warm on a winter ride.

Page 45 As fans press in from every side, Groussard happily doles out autographs to celebrate his win.

Page 46 As was the norm at the now-defunct Bordeaux–Paris, the riders changed out of their "night" clothing at dawn, donning standard race gear for the remainder of the race. At a predetermined location, the riders were met by their teams, given a quick cleanup, and then sent off behind dernys to fight for the finish later that day in Paris.

Page 47 Jesus Galdeano scrapes the snowbank, presumably for refreshment. This group looks like it is just moseying along, but in fact the other riders in the photo are Giorgio Zancanaro (#102), Renzo Fontona (#53), and Guido De Rosso (#82). Zancanaro finished third overall and De Rosso fourth overall. Fontona, no slacker, finished seventh at the 1963 Tour de France.

Page 48 Stage 4 of the 1963 Dauphiné, a 234-km trek from Villard de Lans to Gap, saw reigning world champion Stablinski win a hard-fought battle with Federico Bahamontes, taking victory by a margin of 2 seconds. The next finisher, third place Willy Schroeders, did not arrive for nearly 5 minutes.

Page 49 Rudi Altig's exceptional bike skills enable him to have a relaxing lunch while steering with his left foot and pedaling with his right.

Page 50 Despite the television images of fan-packed roads at the grand tours, riders spend many hours racing on empty roads. This brooding photograph captures such a moment as the peloton works its way through the 1961 Giro.

Page 51 It's often been described as one of the toughest stages of the Giro ever run. This marvelous photo shows Van Looy in his rain jacket as the elder in a group of locals works to ignite a source of heat in the falling snow. The skeptical look on Van Looy's face tells us that if the heater doesn't fire up soon, he's going to head elsewhere for shelter.

Page 52 Another look at the stage 14 finish of the 1962 Giro. Here the legendary French rider Anglade is met by another legend, Jean Bobet, brother of Louison. Note that the snow has started piling up on the hats and shoulders of the soldiers behind Bobet.

Page 53 The Critérium des As was an exciting end-of-season invitational that saw riders behind dernys pedaling furiously in their quest to win. Although the race varied somewhat from year to year, the "standard" length was 100 km, and it often wrapped up in two hours. This photograph captures the unfortunate consequence of following the derny too closely.

Page 54 The Circuit des Boucles de la Seine ran from 1945 to 1973. It followed the twists and turns of the river and was reserved exclusively for French riders. Clearly, it was kinder to some than to others.

Page 55 Desmet, a solid domestique, soldiers on through the miserable stage 14 of the 1962 Giro. Desmet, part of the famous "red guard" of Rik van Looy's Faema-Flandria squad, had a career that spanned the years 1955 to 1967.

Page 56 Bahamontes finds himself isolated during stage 5 of the 1962 Dauphiné Libéré. As evidenced by the number of motos surrounding him, Bahamontes was a popular rider throughout his career. At day's end, the Eagle of Toledo had finished the 214-km stage from Chambéry to Gap in fifth place. He had lost more than 8 minutes to the stage winner, and any chance of taking the overall was dashed. In the end, he finished a respectable fourth overall, a bit over 9 minutes behind race winner Raymond Mastrotto.

Page 57 The sun-splashed beaches at Nice can't arrive quickly enough for this fellow.

Page 58 Bahamontes, the great climber, was a terrible descender. In fact, after leading the charge to the top of a col, he would sometimes wait for other riders to arrive so that he could follow their wheels down the other side. Although Bahamontes remounted and continued after this crash, he was forced to withdraw a few days later, prior to the race finish in Milan.

Page 59 Nencini wears the short-lived but distinct jersey of the race sponsor Moschettieri as he chats with Simpson.

Page 60 Before Twitter, before iPad, before iPhone, Facebook, and Strava, riders had to find other ways to fill the downtime between race stages.

Page 61 Stage 5a of the 1962 Paris–Nice was a 27-km individual time trial (ITT) that turned nasty with the weather. There's nearly as much snow on Geldermans's head as there is on the road.

Page 62 Altig and teammate De Roo lead the charge in a long tradition of pillaging local shopkeepers along the race route. Note that in 1964 the St. Raphaël jerseys still had pockets front and back for maximum load capacity.

Page 63 The look on Assirelli's face tells the story; it followed his bold move earlier in the mountainous 238-km stage. As the first rider to crest Joux, the final climb of the day, Assirelli held off the competition to win by a margin of 35 seconds. He was a career domestique, and this would prove to be his one and only professional victory.

Page 64 The Dauphiné Libéré was important to Anquetil, and he left his mark by winning it five times in his career.

Page 65 Winner of the 1962 French national championship, Stablinski wore the #1 dossard in '63. He repeated his victory by a margin of 25 seconds over Guy Ignolin and 1:24 over third-place Jacques Anquetil. The size of the crowd is mind-boggling.

Page 66 Anquetil had made his dominating move on stage 6a, a 38-km ITT from Avignon to Bollène, to secure the overall lead, a position he would hold to the race's end in Grenoble.

Page 67 The Tour de Var ran for seven years from 1957 to 1963. In its final year, an elated Simpson prevailed to win stage 1 by a margin of 3 seconds over a charging group of five headed by second-place finisher Gilbert Desmet.

Page 68 Anquetil, on the far right, looks like he is in a little difficulty, but his expression is deceptive. He went on to take the overall win.

Page 69 A wonderful candid shot from a stage start. The dress of the fellow on the right suggests that he might be unfamiliar with the complications of the modern safety pin.

Page 70 Poulidor's resignation in his battles with Anquetil is evident. Another tough day, another loss—though Pou-Pou would go on to claim Dauphiné victories in 1966 and 1969.

Page 71 By 1957, in his first Tour de France (which he won by nearly 15 minutes), Anquetil had already set a new hour record (1956) and had won the Grand Prix des Nations four consecutive times (1953–1956). His inclusion on the '57 Tour squad (the Tour was still comprised of national teams) sent the French press into a frenzy, and Anquetil was a willing participant in their photo requests. The utter perfection of this image is due not only to the facial expressions of Anquetil and his autograph seeker but also to the vantage point of the photographer, which allows us to see the ranks of the press competing to get the best shot.

Page 72 With afternoon shadows beginning to stretch across the road, Anquetil's celebrated form could not be more perfect as he powers his way to a win. A truly great photo of a champion at speed.

Page 73 Cynar rider Giuseppe Fezzardi sips an energy drink on his way to a ninth-place finish for stage 10. Fezzardi rode as a professional for 11 seasons; his most notable result was an overall victory at the 1963 Tour de Suisse.

Pages 74–75 The stylish Anquetils were objects of deep fascination for France's press photographers, and the magazines and newspapers of the day vied for exclusive shots of the couple's domestic bliss.

Page 76 After sitting out the 1960 Tour, Anquetil returned in 1961, declaring before the race that he would hold the maillot jaune start to finish. Except for the opening stage, he did, claiming the jersey in the first day's afternoon time trial and wearing it to the end. In 1962, the Tour was raced by trade teams, and though Anquetil fought his team manager, Raphaël Géminiani, and teammate Rudi Altig throughout, he prevailed at the end by luring Federico Bahamontes into a bad strategy. Here we see a confident Anquetil in the yellow jersey at last, which he did not don until stage 20.

Page 77 In 1957, Anquetil won his fifth consecutive Grand Prix des Nations time trial for his Helyett Potin team. In all, he would win the race nine times.

Page 78 A pro for 11 seasons, Dutch rider Jo de Roo was a solid pro whose record includes five grand tour stage victories, two national championships, and six one-day classic wins.

Page 79 As with any race, at the Tour de France there is one winner and one last-place rider. At stage 14 of the 1960 Tour de France, Gastone Nencini was resplendent in yellow while Hans Schleuniger had the distinction of being dead last. By race end, Nencini was the 1960 champion. As for Schleuniger, the yoke of the lanterne rouge was lifted as he ultimately pedaled his way to 80th overall.

Page 80 The beauty of this photo lies almost solely in Graczyk's powerful form, though the expression of the rider behind him will be familiar to anyone who has desperately tried to draft the slipstream of a tornado.

Page 81 Anglade, nicknamed "Napoleon" both for his short stature and his bossy manner, keeps moving down the road toward an eventual eighth-place overall finish.

Page 82 Completely in his element in the final stage, a 12.5-km ITT, Anquetil seals his overall victory over Raymond Poulidor with a commanding first-place performance on the stage. First run in 1932, the Critérium National de la Route was originally a one-day race. Interestingly, the race location changed nearly every year. Beginning in 1963, the year of this photograph, the format was changed to a two-day race comprised of multiple stages. Until 1978, the race was open solely to French riders. In 1979, the name was changed to the Critérium International, the same name used today. Imagine Anquetil's speed were he given one of today's slippery time trial machines to ride.

Page 83 In addition to his riding prowess on the road and track, Bobet was a fairly good cyclocrosser. This unusual photograph, shot from above, shows Bobet clambering up a slippery hillside, seemingly through a thick snare of brambles. They sure don't make cyclocross courses like that anymore.

Page 84 A typical scene along the roads of France in July.

Page 85 Although 1963 fell toward the end of Bahamontes's storied 13-season pro career, it was far from unproductive. He once again won both a stage at the Tour de France and the mountains classification. By the time he retired in 1965, he had won the Tour overall in 1959, captured seven stages, and claimed the mountains jersey six times. In 2013, he was named the best climber in the history of the Tour de France by a prestigious jury appointed by *L'Équipe*.

Page 86 The Tour de l'Avenir was created to showcase the talents of up-and-coming amateurs and semiprofessionals. In particular, it provided an opportunity for riders living in the communist bloc to race in France. Until 1967, it was held on the same days and roads as the Tour de France, albeit with shorter daily stage lengths.

Page 87 Poblet seems outraged by Van Looy's apparent pleasure with a cigarette passed to him—presumably from a team car—by the legendary Gino Bartali. Despite his remarkable racing career and the care he put into his training, Bartali was a lifelong smoker.

Page 88 Two pheasant hunters pause to take in the spectacle of the 1963 Paris–Tours. The romantic glory of *La France profonde* is deeply embedded in French culture, and images like this have long been a comforting sight for traditionalists opposed to the hegemony of Paris.

Page 89 Imagine the surprise for this family, dressed for a day at the Tour de France, when star rider Jan Janssen, center in glasses, stopped by for a quick drink!

Page 90 The crowning achievement of Beheyt's seven-year professional career was his unexpected victory at the 1963 world championships. His win was not without significant controversy. As the field hurtled down the finishing straight, fellow Belgian Rik van Looy was at the front with just meters to go and looked poised for victory. Beheyt, sitting on Van Looy's wheel, raced up beside him, grabbed his jersey, and slipped by to win the race. While Van Looy took the slight in stride at the race, he later made it clear he would not look favorably at any team or race organizer that helped Beheyt. Aside from a stage victory at the 1964 Tour de France, there were no more significant wins for Beheyt. With little support from fellow riders and few options for spots on teams, Beheyt retired in 1968 at the young age of 27.

Page 91 Poulidor remains a fan favorite in France. He was a true all-rounder whose road season started in the early spring and did not finish until the Giro di Lombardia. Here we see another marvelous Carpano team car; note the cut-down window for the mechanic.

Page 92 It's early in the day on a flat sector, and Tour director Goddet is urging his troops on, almost certainly to their annoyance.

Page 93 Stage 10 was a split day, with a road stage from Monaco to Hyères in the morning (won by Jan Janssen) and an ITT from Hyères to Toulon in the afternoon (won by Jacques Anquetil). In between, an enterprising photographer captured this image.

Page 94 This wonderfully composed photograph captures a routine wheel change with near perfection. The rider, Nencini, patiently waits as his mechanic swaps out a front wheel. The team car sits just to the left in all its 1950s glory. The looming clouds and desolate landscape add to the rider's sense of isolation from the disappearing peloton ahead.

Page 95 While there actually is a thin trickle of oil dripping from the can spout, the real purpose of this visit to the team car is easy to judge from two clues: One, the rider's right hand is firmly planted on the car fender, and two, if this were a real mechanical, surely the aid would come from a backseat mechanic, not the driver!

Page 96 Wearing the maillot jaune he had captured only two days prior, Anquetil is off and rolling on the 54.5-km ITT. By the early '60s, virtually all of the press photographers and videographers (there's one at left in this photo) had abandoned follow cars for motos, allowing the race to squeeze more coverage onto its tight roads.

Page 97 A competent climber, Uliana seized his opportunity for victory and was first to crest the first of two climbs that day. Although race leader Hans Junkermann would lead the second ascent, Uliana prevailed to win the stage.

Page 98 Adorni crushed his competition at the 1968 world's at Imola, Italy. While 84 riders started, only 19 finished. His margin of 9:50 over second-place Herman van Springel is the largest in the history of the championships.

Page 99 The 1962 Vuelta, 17 stages over 2,814 km, had an average speed of 36.17 km/h, which may have contributed to this rider's distress.

Page 100 Reigning world champion Beheyt shows the pain of the race as he grinds his way to the velodrome in Roubaix. While he was unable to overtake Rik van Looy, he did get a place on the podium's second step.

Page 101 Pambianco is about to shove that newspaper under his jersey to block the wind on his descent. The Gavia was the last major climb of the 1960 Giro d'Italia, and this stage was the last shot the contenders had to unseat the maglia rosa, Jacques Anquetil. Anquetil, however, would not be denied, as the 3:41 he lost on the stage was not enough to knock him from the lead. For his effort, Pambianco finished seventh overall. He exacted his revenge the following year, beating second-place Anquetil by 3:45 to become the Giro's 1961 champion.

Page 102 And some say winning isn't everything.

Page 103 You can't finish the Tour without dedicated support.

Page 104 The Circuit Daumesnil was a 50-km race done partially behind dernys. It took a bit over one hour to complete and was often filled with top-name stars. In 1959, Darrigade finished third behind race winner Dominique Forlini and Miguel Poblet.

Page 105 Nineteen sixty-nine was Anquetil's final year as a pro cyclist. It was also a spectacular year for the new superstar Eddy Merckx. As Coppi (page 6) defined his era and Anquetil the next, Merckx would become the supernova by which all other athletes—cyclists and otherwise—would forever be compared. Anquetil and Merckx shared a professional respect that continued to the day Anquetil died in 1987.

Page 106 At the end of the day, three things are certain: The riders need to be fed, the bikes need to be fettled, and someone needs to wash the kit. The composition of this photo could not be more perfect, from the symmetry of the jerseys on the lines to the shadows they cast in the courtyard.

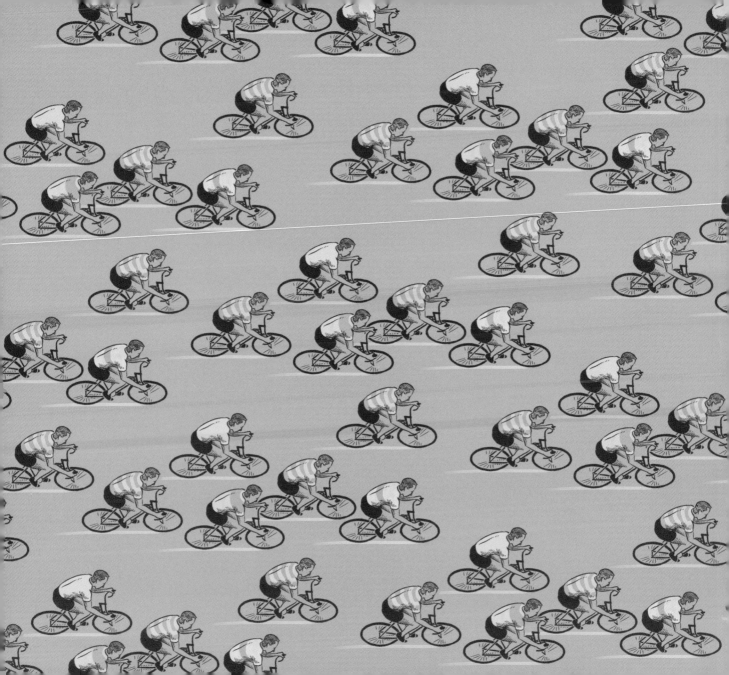